Fire! Fire!

Redvers Brandling

Illustrated by Donald Harley

The Great Fire of London, 1666

Basil Blackwell

London's burning, London's burning,
Fetch the engine, fetch the engine,
Fire, fire; Fire, fire;
Pour on water, pour on water.

It was September 1st, 1666.
John Farynor was very tired.
"It's been a long day," he thought, as
he climbed upstairs to bed, in his
room above the baker's
shop in London's Pudding Lane.
John was royal baker to the
King of England, King Charles II.
To be the royal baker was a great
honour, but it meant that he
had to work very hard.
John was so tired that night that he
forgot to do something very important.
Downstairs in his baker's ovens
a flame still flickered.
John had forgotten to
damp down his ovens.

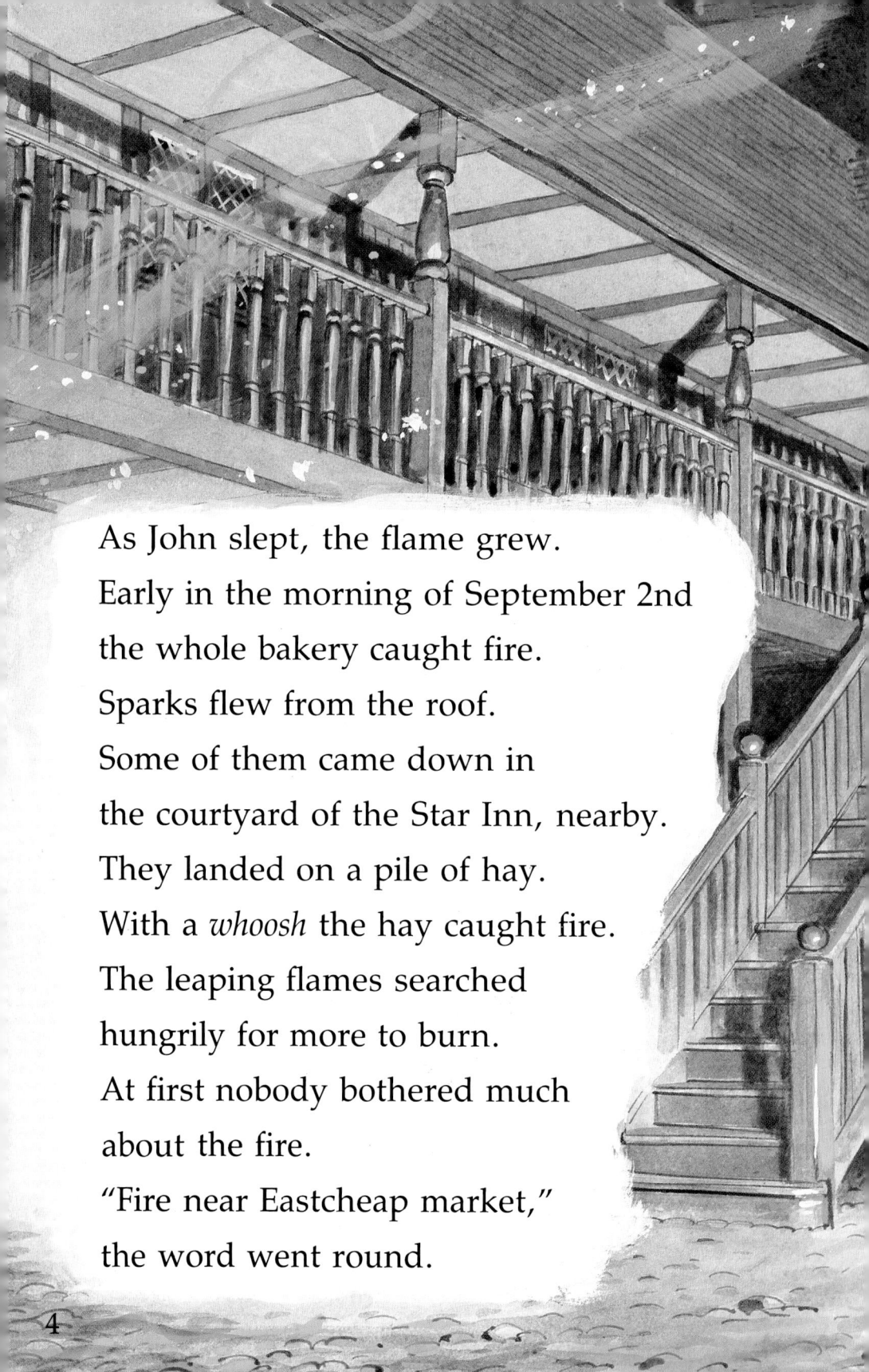

As John slept, the flame grew.
Early in the morning of September 2nd
the whole bakery caught fire.
Sparks flew from the roof.
Some of them came down in
the courtyard of the Star Inn, nearby.
They landed on a pile of hay.
With a *whoosh* the hay caught fire.
The leaping flames searched
hungrily for more to burn.
At first nobody bothered much
about the fire.
"Fire near Eastcheap market,"
the word went round.

People left their homes and came to watch.
"It's a fair old blaze."
"Oh, there's one every few weeks in this part of London.
They never amount to much."
No-one tried to put the flames out.

The fire began to spread. It reached the main road to London Bridge.

A message was sent to the Mayor. "Just another fire," he snorted, and said some rude things to the people who had got him out of bed. Still nothing was done about it.

One wooden house after another burst into flames.

The blaze swept on its way to the River Thames.

When it reached the river a dry wind from the east blew the flames towards a line of warehouses. The first one held timber. It was soon blazing. Then the second one caught fire. It was full of brandy and exploded like a great bomb. The next had coal. It sent out a tremendous heat as it burned.

At last people realised that this fire would not die out on its own. An official called Samuel Pepys went to see King Charles.

"Your Majesty," said Samuel, "London is on fire – we must do something about it."

"On fire? On fire?" replied the King. "Nobody has told me anything about it."

"Look," said Samuel.

He pointed out of the window.

Great clouds of smoke were
rising over the River Thames.
"What has the Mayor done about this?"
asked the King.
"Nothing, your Majesty."
"What!" stormed the King.
"Only last year I told him to take
more care about fires.
We must act at once."

Fire fighters were sent to try to
stop the blaze.
But they made a bad mistake.
They hacked open the water
pipes to fill their buckets more quickly
The water ran away – then the
supply dried up.

Now the fire was like a monster.
Its fiery breath was everywhere.
Shops on London Bridge crackled and soon the banks of the Thames were ablaze.

☐ Area affected by the fire
✱ John Farynor's baker's shop

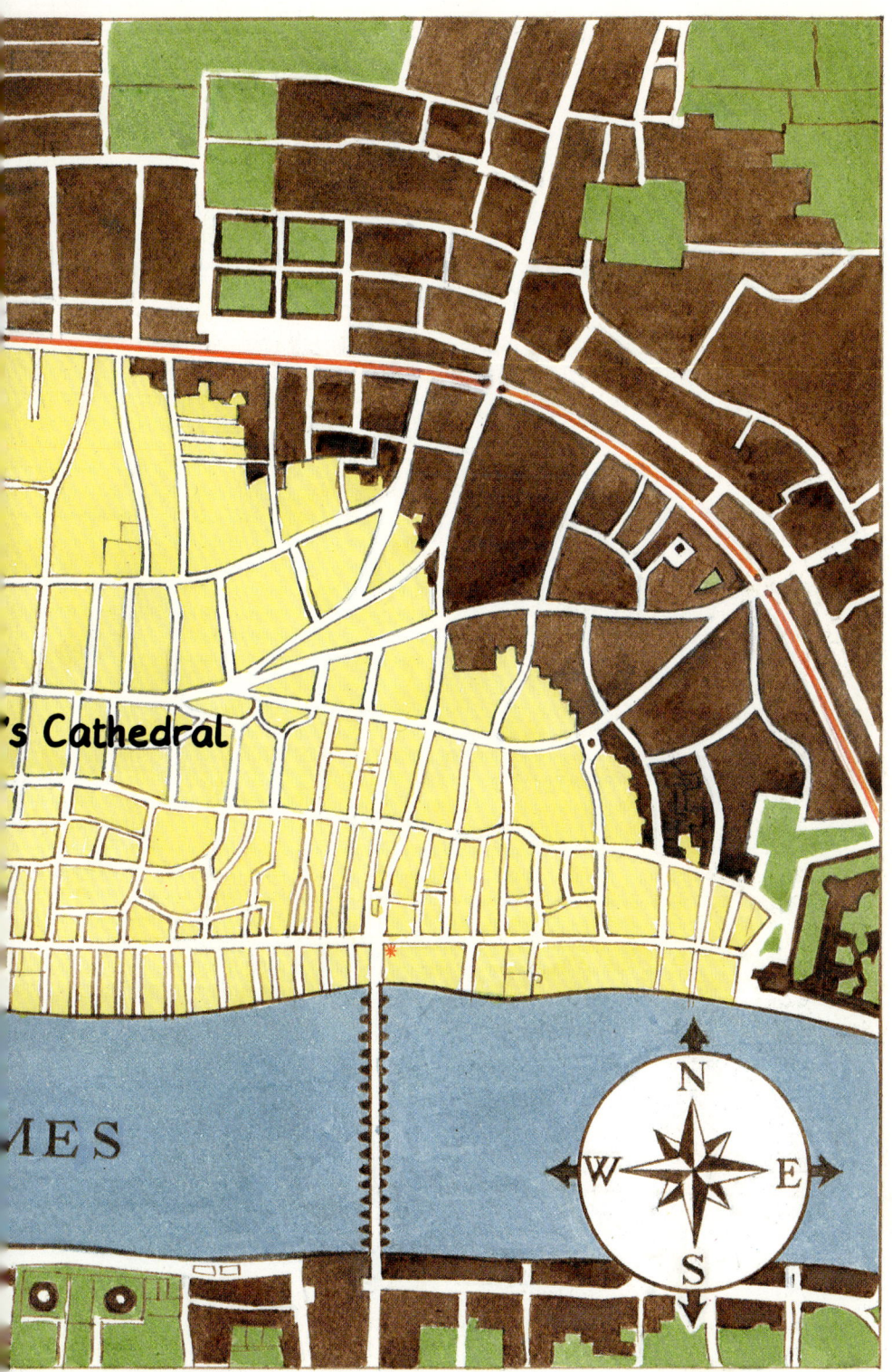

St Paul's Cathedral was like a
huge bonfire.
Explosions blew great
holes in the stonework.
Tombs burst open.
The roof melted and red-hot lead ran
down the streets.
Men, women and children
snatched up their belongings and ran.
Some people rushed to the River
Thames and crowded into boats.

Monday 3rd September
It was hard to tell whether it
was day or night.
Huge, choking clouds of
smoke covered the sun.
The fire burned on and on.
Two thousand houses . . . five
thousand houses . . . ten thousand
houses . . .
Ten, twenty, thirty, forty churches.

Tuesday 4th September
Now the wind got up.
The wind blew sparks from
the fire over the City.
Some of the sparks blew towards
the Tower of London.
"If that catches fire
there will be nothing left,"
said Jem, a sailor in a ship on the Thames.

"Why?" asked Ben, one of his shipmates. "Because it's crammed full of gunpowder," went on Jem. "Remember we unloaded our cargo near there the other day? A docker told me what was in the Tower. If the fire takes hold of it, there will be the biggest bang the world has ever heard!"

Now King Charles decided to take charge.
He knew there was only one thing to do.
"It's no good trying to put out
the fire," he said.
"We've got to knock down buildings so
that there is nothing for it to burn."
The fire fighters planted explosives
in the houses in the path of the fire.
They lit the fuses and rushed to safety.

Boom!
The houses were blown to pieces.
Great gaps appeared in front of
the blaze.
The flames reached out hungrily for
more to burn, but there was nothing there.
The Tower was saved.

Wednesday 5th September

At last the fire had stopped spreading. It still leapt and scorched and roared, but the rest of London was safe.

On Thursday the wind died down.

"We're winning!" shouted the fire fighters.

"We've got it under control."

A dreadful smell of burning hung over the city.
Flames still crackled in ruins and cellars.
Some of these fires went on burning for six months.
But the worst of the fire was over.

Now people began to look at the damage.
Over thirteen thousand houses had
been destroyed.
One hundred thousand people had
lost their homes and all they owned.
Most had only been able to save
a few clothes.
Eighty-seven churches had gone.
Where St Paul's had stood, nothing
was left.
Nothing but ruins.

But in some ways the fire had done London a good turn. The germs of the Great Plague, a disease which had killed thousands of people the year before, were wiped out. New houses were built, but this time many were made of stone, which would not burn. In a few years London began to grow again, into a safer and more beautiful city.

We know so much about the fire of London because two men who lived at the time kept diaries.
Their names were Samuel Pepys and John Evelyn.
In his diary, John wrote that he saw 'ten thousand houses all in one flame'.
Samuel said that 'If at any time the sun peeped forth it looked red like blood'.
What a terrible sight the Great Fire must have been.